D0975307

# IN CONCLUSION, DON'T WORRY ABOUT IT

BALLANTINE BOOKS | NEW YORK

# LAUREN GRAHAM

# IN CONCLUSION, DON'T WORRY ABOUT IT

Published in the United States by Ballantine Books, an imprint
of Random House, a division of Penguin Random House LLC,
New York.

BALLANTINE and the HOUSE colophon are registered trademarks
of Penguin Random House LLC.

LIBRARY OF CONGRESS CATALOGING-IN-PUBLICATION DATA
Names: Graham, Lauren, author.
Title: In conclusion, don't worry about it / Lauren Graham.
Description: First edition. | New York : Ballantine Books, 2018. |
Expanded version of the author's 2017 commencement speech at
her hometown Langley High School (Virginia).
Identifiers: LCCN 2017061314| ISBN 9781524799595 (hardcover :
alk. paper) | ISBN 9781524799601 (ebook)
Subjects: LCSH: Self-actualization (Psychology) | Success—
Psychological aspects. | Conduct of life.
Classification: LCC BF637.S4 G7333 2018 | DDC 170/.44—dc23
LC record available at https://lccn.loc.gov/2017061314

Printed in the United States of America on acid-free paper

randomhousebooks.com

9 8 7 6 5 4 3 2 1

FIRST EDITION

Book design by Simon M. Sullivan

To graduates and other hopefuls

# INTRODUCTION

"CONGRATULATIONS! You're giving the graduation speech at Langley High School this year," my dad told me as we bounced down a windy Virginia road in his open-air Jeep. Windy road plus bouncy car plus hair whipping in my face had me jangled, and I wasn't sure I was hearing him properly.

"I'm doing the—what?" I asked him. Did I apply for this? I thought to myself. Is it possible I forgot I'd said yes to giving the commencement speech at my alma mater? The way my dad put it, it seemed like the happy outcome of some contest, but it was one I didn't remember entering.

"Remember Dick, who I play tennis with?"

"No?"

"You know. Dick? From tennis."

"I—no, I don't, Dad."

"Well, his granddaughter Kaitlin is graduating from Langley."

"Uh-huh."

"And you're giving the speech! Isn't that great?" he said, as if it was all settled. And while I was sure there was a chink in his logic somewhere—perhaps due to the potholes that kept jogging me out of my seat—I couldn't find it, and by the time we arrived home, my hair a tangled mess, I had somehow become a commencement speaker.

As an actor, I'd performed in front of an audience many times before, but I'd never exactly "spoken" to one. So I asked for advice.

"Open with a joke," my dad—an experienced public speaker in his capacity as president of a company for over twenty years—told me. "Don't talk as fast as you normally do," friends advised. "Have you seen Will Ferrell's commencement address? Now *that's* a good speech," said literally every other person I asked. He'd given a speech at USC that year that was, indeed, hilarious. He sang. It went viral. WHATEVER, WILL.

After I gave the speech to the Langley graduates, I was asked to publish it. "Are you going to make it funnier? Like that Will Ferrell speech?" people asked me when I told them the news.

So, this book started with the Langley speech, but grew considerably from there. I kept thinking of all the worrying I'd done when confronted with milestone moments in life, how generally unhelpful worry is, and how much admiration I have for the young people I've gotten to meet over the years. We desperately need your talent, your integrity, and your hope. If this book helps you worry even slightly less as you navigate your future, I'll be thrilled.

Recently, I was asked to speak to the students at University College Dublin. They probably heard about my Langley speech, I congratulated myself. I'm probably going to become a very big-deal world-renowned public speaker of some sort. I hope I have enough time to work on my—

Then I did some more research.

Their speaker from last year? WILL FER-RELL. He wore their national football uniform. He painted himself green from head to toe. Whatever. I'M GONNA GET YOU, WILL.

Honestly? I can't wait to hear how funny he was from folks with that charming Irish lilt.

# IN CONCLUSION, DON'T WORRY ABOUT IT

I graduated from high school in 1984. Back then, a movie ticket cost about three dollars, the Apple Macintosh computer had just come out, and *Ghostbusters* (with dudes) was the top-grossing movie. No one I knew had a cellphone, our high school didn't have a marching band, and that year, our class didn't have a graduation speaker either —in another three decades a robot will dispense wisdom via satellite from space, or from one of those islands Richard Branson owns, and you'll watch it on the drone projector in your safe house! (Apologies if my sophisticated comprehension of the future of technology goes over your head.)

I don't remember much about my graduation ceremony. It was just too hard for me to focus. I was wearing a scratchy white dress. It was hot outside, and even stuffier under the polyester robes. We barely had any good hair products back then and my hair was always poofy. I was wearing heels I'd never worn before and they'd given me a blister. We were seated alphabetically, and I didn't know the students who sat to my left or right. My close friends were scattered somewhere across the auditorium, but I couldn't see any of them. Everything felt off, and strange, and muggy.

Even having my diploma in hand felt sort of like an empty victory. Well, not sort of, since due to library fines my diploma was being held, and the pleather envelope I received after I shook hands with the principal was *actually* empty. Inside was just a blank piece of paper. No name, no date, no year. My diploma would be held hostage until I returned my long overdue copy of *Robinson Crusoe*. I was somehow both overwhelmed and scattered, far from focused on my future.

On that graduation day, I could see about as clearly as "Will Cindy's older brother buy us enough wine coolers for the party tonight?" You know, deep, intellectual stuff. So, if you're worried that—at the end of high school, or college, or even a long relationship— you're supposed to know more about what comes next than whatever the Bartles & Jaymes count at the next party is, don't worry about it! Thresholds/passages/finales of any kind tend to have a forced, fake-cheery, New Year's Eve–type pressure about them. An ISN'T THIS AMAZING, I'VE GOT IT ALL FIGURED OUT-ness that isn't true for everyone. And like on New Year's Eve, some people have a detailed plan involving light-up hats and elaborate outfits and going to Times Square, while some just want to stay home and hide under a blanket. Neither method of handling a supposed "big" life moment guarantees what the future will bring. Both are valid choices.

Except going to Times Square on New Year's. I mean that's just nuts.

In high school, I dreamed of one day becoming a professional actor, but had no idea how or if or when that could ever happen. So, in the meantime, I auditioned for school plays. In my freshman year, I was cast as Townsperson #3 in the spring musical, *Li'l Abner*. I was thrilled to be part of the company and to have any role at all. Sophomore year, I was the understudy for the lead in *Anything Goes,* and I was as proud as I'd ever been the night I got to play Reno Sweeney, even though it was just a rehearsal, and even though the audience was comprised of only a few stagehands and a smattering of my fellow company members waiting for their cues.

It was during my junior year that I was cast as Dolly in *Hello, Dolly!,* my first leading role, and I loved every minute of it. To this day, my father still gets a faraway, misty look when he talks about my performance. "A standing ovation! All three nights!" he'll say, to anyone who'll listen. Even if gently reminded that I've had a few acting jobs since then, for him, nothing has had quite the staying power of that year's accomplishment.

The musical my senior year was *Once Upon a Mattress,* a comedic adaptation of *The Princess and the Pea,* in which there were not one but two excellent leading roles. Friends rolled their eyes when I expressed any concern over the audition. *"Please,"* they told me. "It's a no-brainer. The only question is *which* part you want."

I was strangely nervous the day of the audition. Rather than feeling hopeful, as I had the year before, I felt pressure to succeed. Maybe that's the reason that when I opened my mouth to sing, I was off. My voice broke where it shouldn't have, and I began to lose confidence. I finished, but I never recovered. My teacher looked solemn as I exited. He'd asked us beforehand to write on our audition forms whether we were interested only in lead roles or if we'd accept any part. I checked the box marked "any part." I thought it seemed tacky to suggest I was above any role, especially since before I walked into the room, I'd felt pretty sure of myself.

I didn't get either of the two leads. Instead, I was cast as a lady-in-waiting. It was a speaking part, but I don't think the character even had a name. I could have probably bowed out, but my pride dictated that I stay in the show—it felt like I'd been demoted, but I couldn't go back on the box I'd checked. One day, I heard my teacher whispering something about a "senior slump" and saw him looking my way. *Was that it?* I wondered to myself. One year of accomplishment followed immediately by a slump year? Would I ever come out of it, or was the rest of my life slump-bound? Was junior year's success a fluke, or was this year's setback a sign of things to come?

On the way to the show on opening night, my car slid on a patch of ice on Georgetown Pike and went off the road. I was fine, but my car had to be towed and I arrived at school in a police car. My drama teacher met me in the green room. "Are you okay?" he asked. "Are you going to be able to go on tonight?" I paused for a second and allowed myself a moment of relief. Maybe I didn't have to do this after all. Maybe I'd unintentionally found a way out. Maybe I *was* in a slump and the best thing to do would be to just give in to it and go home.

Then I felt a tap on my shoulder. It was Jenny, a pretty, blond sophomore who had a small, nonspeaking role. "Lauren?" she said, her blue eyes round with sympathy. "I heard what happened. I'm *so* sorry. I want you to know that if you can't do the show to-night . . ." She paused, and her eyes narrowed just the slightest bit. "I can go on for you. I can go on, because *I've learned all your lines.*"

Suddenly, I snapped out of it. Suddenly, I was okay. My shattered nerves turned steely and I took my first deep breath since the accident. Looking into Jenny's eyes I saw ambition and fire and determination. I recognized myself. To me, my role was a demotion, but Jenny still aspired to get there one day. "I'll be fine, thanks," I said in a voice that surprised me. I sounded calm.

In the end, I went on, although it was hard to shake the disappointed feeling, the feeling that I'd let myself down somehow. I'm sure I looked at the girls with bigger parts that night just the way Jenny looked at me in the green room. My small role was giving me a sad heart. Was the secret to happiness a simple matter of getting The Most? The most lines, the most costume changes, the most applause? Was that all it was? It sort of felt that way that night, but I wondered . . .

I tell you these stories because when I look back, I still think of My Life in High School Musical Theater as a metaphor for pretty much everything that was to follow in the "real" world. I've had ups and downs. I've had successes and senior slumps. I've been the girl who has the lead, and the one who wished she had the bigger part. The truth? They don't feel that different from each other.

My happiness has not been found in Mosts or Bests, no matter how many times I expected to find it there. And I've looked, believe me. Once in a while, I still look. We're all told it's there, all the time—why else have awards and games and reality shows that crown a winner? If it isn't The Best to publicly win at things, then what *is* The Best, where is it, and how can I get some?

I continued my search.

YEARS after I graduated from high school, I finally achieved the dream I'd had when I first started out as Townsperson #3 in *L'il Abner*. I made it to Broadway, where I got to play Miss Adelaide in the revival of *Guys and Dolls*. A proven crowd-pleaser of a show, a gem of a role. Surely, this had to be one of the Best of the Bests out there. What could possibly go wrong? Lots of things, it turns out. There was the memory in New York of the last revival, which had been both critically beloved and a huge commercial hit. To separate our production from that one, decisions were made to reflect the current grim economic climate in tone and set design. "Bleak *Guys and Dolls*?

I'm not sure," a director friend said to me after an early preview.

And then there was confidence, my old friend/foe. I'd been a professional actor for years at this point. Surely I'd figured out the secret to it by now? As it turned out, I hadn't. The pressure I put on myself was immense. From the moment rehearsals began, I worried about *everything*. Was I good enough? Did I deserve to be there? An actor friend came to an early preview. "You're doing what's required, but something's missing," he told me. "You don't seem free. You aren't *starring* in it yet." Well, of course I wasn't doing anything as audacious as *starring* in the show. How could I, when I was so certain I didn't deserve to be there in the first place? I couldn't quite allow myself the freedom to enjoy it when I was so sure I was an impostor.

Then, some nights everything would mysteriously click. And I'd try to repeat whatever I thought that winning combination was, but I'd fail to find it the next night. I was wracked with anxiety. Within a single week of performances, I cycled through the same waves I'd experienced in high school, only more concentrated. Certain nights were *Hello, Dolly!*, others felt like a senior slump. I couldn't figure out what the difference between them was. It felt like my performance was controlling me, rather than the other way around.

But as the weeks passed, I began to hit my stride. It was too late in one way—the reviews had already come out, which meant all the "important" people had already made their judgments. But the timing was perfect in another way. Finally, I had stopped caring who exactly was in the audience. No matter who they were, I realized they were just hoping for a good time and a few laughs, and they deserved to get it. What they hadn't paid for was to see me worried that I wasn't living up to my own idea of who I was supposed to be. So I decided to stop worrying altogether. I decided to bring joy with me onstage every night, even the ones when it felt like the audience was comprised entirely of coughers and candy unwrappers and theater critics. And a funny thing happened: Once I stopped worrying so much about pleasing others, once I decided to let myself off the hook, I realized I could fly.

"What happened to you?" the same friend who'd seen the early preview asked, and I struggled to articulate the change.

"I don't know," I told him. "But it sort of feels like . . . sailing."

You've felt it too, haven't you? Even for a fleeting moment? When you're engrossed in a good book, or losing yourself in trying a new recipe, or tackling something at work, and then you look up at the clock, only to realize just how many hours have passed. Whatever you want to call it: flying, sailing, surfing. It's the way time moves differently when you're caught up in the simple joy of being yourself. It's what can happen when you make the decision to let go of criticism and worry and fear.

And that's where The Best really lives.

BACK on this day in 1984, if you had to guess who'd be giving the graduation speech in 2017, you'd have named thirty to four hundred people before you got to me.

So if you're kicking yourself for not having accomplished all you thought you should have by now, don't worry about it. People bloom at different stages of their lives, and often more than once. My dad ran a successful company for years, then, at age 72, became a certified spinning instructor because he loved cycling so much. (Although this certification only took three days, which—I'm not saying *don't* take his class? But maybe give it a few more weeks.)

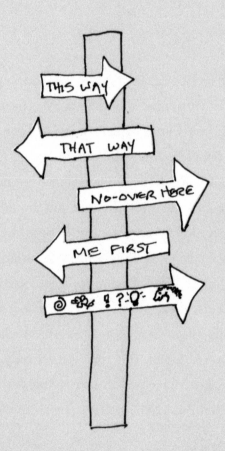

Eventually, I was lucky enough to have the career I wanted, but it wasn't a straight shot or an easy path; it was a series of ups and downs, of steps forward and then back again. I've experienced setbacks where I've allowed myself to get angry and feel hurt. I've had disappointments and put the focus on someone else in an attempt to feel better: "Hey, how did Biffles Schniffelson get the thing I wanted?" (I just made Biffles up. Insert your nemesis here.) "Biffles Schniffelson doesn't deserve it/didn't work as hard/already has *so much*—isn't it my turn? Why wasn't it me?"

You may feel these emotions in the face of disappointment—you may have a *right* to, in fact. You can probably find friends and relatives to agree with your feelings of injustice, too. "You *do* deserve it! It should have been you! If I have to see another Biffles Schniffelson movie, I'll just barf!" You might walk around angry for a while, might lose your inspiration, or try to drown your sorrows. "I hate you, Biffelth!" you might hiccup into your beer—or worse, into your Snapchat. You may be right that you've been wronged— you may even be *one hundred percent correct* in your assessment of the world as an unfair place.

BUT here's a secret: The lows don't last any longer than the highs do. Like clouds on an overcast day, sometimes we have to face the fact that what happens to us in life isn't controllable, and if we wait a while, don't take it personally, and decide to enjoy ourselves anyway, the sky will eventually clear up.

It always does.

Then, one day, it'll finally be your turn. After all the hard work and hoping and dreaming, the winner will be *you*. Maybe you got the most praise, or the biggest raise, or the part in that movie that Biffles Schniffelson was after. Hooray! Now all the problems and mixed feelings and fatigue and anxiety on the way to winning will magically melt in the warmth of the praise and awards and accolades, and maybe even money that comes with being a winner, right? And once you get there, there'll be no more insecurity. You'll finally make peace with the confidence that's sometimes eluded you, because success makes confidence your friend for life, doesn't it?

Well, sort of.

THE truth is, achieving success doesn't automatically bring you confidence. And coming in ahead of Biffles Schniffelson will only make you feel better for an annoyingly brief moment. Satisfaction is not found in the big achievements. It's not in winning. Starring has nothing to do with how big your part is—it's a state of mind.

I have one of those dream jobs that people assume must contain an incredible amount of joy. And it does. But not always in the ways you might think. The best parts of my job are usually the ones you never see. I'm thrilled every time I step onto a soundstage in the morning. I never open one of those heavy stage doors without thinking: *Really? I get to work here? This is my actual job?* Those doors open onto a dark stage, and as my eyes adjust, I hear the crew barking directions to one another, hanging lights, and toting ladders—sounds that are as cheery to me as Christmas bells. I somehow never tire of the inevitably mediocre coffee from craft service, because it's

BOOKS!
DOGS!
MUSIC!
NEW SNEAKERS!
TREES!
KISSING!
BRUNCH!
SOME CATS!
LOOK UP!

a reminder that I get to be a part of a hard-working group whose shared goal is to tell a story that hopefully entertains people. Walking onto the re-created set of Lorelai's house after all those years was one of the biggest thrills of my life. The fun of doing the daily crossword puzzle with my TV children between shots on the set of *Parenthood* rivaled any awards show I've ever attended. The "success" parts of life look good to others, but the best parts are actually the simple, daily experiences. This is true whether you're an actor or a teacher or a waitress. I know this because I've been all three.

When you finally achieve one of your goals—which you will—and at long last get to a place you dreamed of for years, and it doesn't exactly feel the way you hoped it would, don't worry about it. I've had few achievements that felt much better than morning crew sounds and crossword puzzles with friends and middling coffee made with love. Because the spotlight aspect of life? That's not the satisfying part. In my career, I've been in the spotlight at times, and it was . . . perfectly adequate! It was just fine. It was something, but it wasn't everything.

It took me a long time to understand that it's pretty much just as fun to be Townsperson #3, with no pressure and nothing to prove. There's not as much glory perhaps, but there's the pure enjoyment of getting to be part of something you love. The truth is, you're not a better or happier person when you're Dolly in *Hello, Dolly!*—it just looks that way to others. In real life, I've found progress lives in small and seemingly uneventful accomplishments: the homework you finished, the journal you remembered to write in, the same run you took on the same path as yesterday.

These things might not always seem like much, but over time, they add up to something

bigger. They become the foundation of your life, building blocks on the way to all those milestone moments. It's undeniably fun to call your parents and tell them someone noticed you in a measurable way: a good grade, a raise, some positive feedback. Or to get recognized by others on the "big" days, like when you get into college or find your first job. Or, of course, when you graduate. But those days are few and far more rare than the many, many more days when you and your work will go unnoticed. In the meantime, perform every job as if you're being well paid, as someone who probably wasn't paying me well once told me. Which is to say: why not treat yourself now as the success you dream of becoming? Respect yourself and your work as you would if you were being paid to be the boss, and I bet you'll climb the ladder even faster.

MAYBE it's not acting for you. Maybe it's baseball or coding or taking care of kids. But whatever path you choose, whatever career you decide to go after, the important thing is that you keep finding joy in what you're doing, especially when the joy isn't finding you. Treat every day like you're starring in it. Don't wait for permission or good reviews. If you can do that, you'll be surprised by how far you might end up sailing.

NOT too long ago, I got to see *Hello, Dolly!* on Broadway. I was sitting next to my dad in the theater, and when the lights went down and the overture began, I was surprised to feel tears spring up at the sound of such cheery music. Hearing the orchestra play brought back so many memories of high school, of a time when I was thrilled to be onstage in any capacity at all, full of hope mixed with the fear of not knowing whether my small successes in school would ever translate meaningfully in the real world. I knew I'd feel nostalgic, but I didn't expect to be so emotional. Still, I figured I'd settle down once the show began.

I was wrong.

I'm pretty sure I cried through the whole thing. All the people in my row were probably elbowing one another in frustration: "Doesn't that girl know it's a comedy?" But here's why . . .

I don't know that I've ever experienced a more exuberant production. Watching Bette Midler play the lead confirmed everything I've ever suspected about the transformative power of joy. You couldn't not be transfixed by watching her. She was gleeful, she was funny, she sailed, she surfed, she soared, she *starred* in a way I'll be trying and probably failing to emulate for the rest of my life. Beanie Feldstein shined with such humor and warmth in what's usually considered a supporting part but didn't feel that way at all this time. The entire company was radiant. I bet not one person goes home with the "Jenny look" in their

eyes, because they're *all* the stars of the show. They already have The Most. But they're not waiting for it to be given to them; they're bringing it themselves. And that's the secret to pretty much everything.

DON'T wait until you're on Broadway. Or until you reach the Olympics. Or until you're CEO of a major company. Don't wait until you're the president of something, or for the day when your life looks perfect to you and everyone you know. As I like to say: "Have no fear of perfection—you'll never reach it." Just kidding, that's a quote from Salvador Dali. I do however like to tell people, especially regarding writing and deadlines: "Don't be perfect, just be done." Which is yet another way of saying: "Don't worry so much."

Love yourself, and what you're doing, even if you're not yet at the place you hope to land. Let joy be the thing that drives you, and I bet you'll get there faster. Give yourself permission to make mistakes. Those mistakes are as valuable as the triumphs. If you free yourself from having to be "right," you'll open so many doors. You might choose classes that interest you, rather than ones you're "supposed" to take. You might carry a book with you that isn't something you're required to read for school. You might try something new—like, say, taking a three-day spinning instructor certification class—and change direction entirely. And why not? Your job doesn't define you—your bravery and kindness and gratitude do. Even without any "big" accomplishments yet to your name, you are enough. Whether you have top billing, or you're still dancing in the back row, you are enough, just as you are.

In conclusion, don't worry about it.

You already have The Most. And you're already one of The Best.

## ACKNOWLEDGMENTS

THANKS as always to Esther Newberg, Jennifer E. Smith, Sara Weiss, and the early readers at Random House: Elana Seplow-Jolley, Anne Speyer, and Hanna Gibeau. Thanks to the Langley High School Class of 2017, who inspired the speech that became this book, and thanks to my dad for signing me up for things and informing me about them later, a tendency that's sometimes daunting, but never not fun.

## ABOUT THE AUTHOR

LAUREN GRAHAM is an actor, writer, and producer best known for her roles on the critically acclaimed series *Gilmore Girls* and *Parenthood*. She is also the *New York Times* bestselling author of *Someday, Someday, Maybe* and *Talking as Fast as I Can*. Graham has performed on Broadway and appeared in such films as *Bad Santa*, *Because I Said So*, and *Max*. She holds a BA in English from Barnard College and an MFA in acting from Southern Methodist University. She lives in New York and Los Angeles.

Twitter: @thelaurengraham

## ABOUT THE TYPE

This book was set in Bembo, a typeface based on an old-style Roman face that was used for Cardinal Pietro Bembo's tract *De Aetna* in 1495. Bembo was cut by Francesco Griffo (1450–1518) in the early sixteenth century for Italian Renaissance printer and publisher Aldus Manutius (1449–1515). The Lanston Monotype Company of Philadelphia brought the well-proportioned letterforms of Bembo to the United States in the 1930s.